Law Enforcement
and
AIDS

Questions of Justice and Care

Gad J. Bensinger, Ph.D.
Cyprian Rowe, M.S.W., Ph.D.

Loyola University of Chicago

Published by Loyola University of Chicago
820 N. Michigan Avenue, Room 715
Chicago, IL   60611

Designed by The Center for Instructional Design
Loyola University of Chicago

ISBN 0-942854-13-6

Acknowledgments

This publication could not have been produced without the cooperation of the various presenters and the assistance provided by Loyola University's Center for Instructional Design. We are grateful for the help extended to us by the many individuals involved in the production of this publication.

Gad J. Bensinger
Cyprian L. Rowe
February, 1988

Table of Contents

Introduction

On Wednesday, October 21, 1987, Loyola University of Chicago sponsored a conference titled "Law Enforcement and AIDS: Questions of Justice and Care," which was organized by the Department of Criminal Justice and the School of Social Work. The National Institute of Corrections of the U.S. Department of Justice also assisted in this endeavor.

The purpose of the conference was to bring together representatives from the courts, court services, probation departments, local police departments, corrections and other public service agencies to discuss the issue of AIDS in their worksettings. The areas in which they serve are most difficult, as they deal with those breaches in the public order where lives are thrown into conflict.

In a recent article titled "The AIDS Dilemma" and subtitled "Lawmakers and Lobbyists Try to Please Everyone But Satisfy No One," we read the following:

...The AIDS debate carries with it not only a concern about a deadly epidemic but the potential to affect social policy through the rest of the 20th Century and beyond. At its political core, it is a struggle between factions seeking to preserve the status quo or assert their agenda upon the nation. (Kass & Daley, Chicago Tribune, *9-6-87)*

We at Loyola see it as our role to foster participation in the ongoing national dialogue on AIDS – an issue of such ramifications that it touches and challenges every one of us with regard to our moral and social, political and economic, medical and educational values.

For this dialogue the organizers brought together a number of men and women who are servants of the public order. They were encouraged to share, challenge, suggest, describe and discuss a number of issues pertaining to the many aspects of the AIDS dilemma as it relates to law enforcement, legal, medical, social, pastoral and personal perspectives on AIDS.

Following the conference it was decided that the presentations of the speakers ought to be shared and made available to a wider audience. Consequently, this document and a videotape of the conference's highlights were produced.

The organizers' intent was that all participants in this conference would carry on an internal dialogue and carry back to their respective agencies the principal ideas concerning the issues of justice and care. It was also hoped that this conference would reveal not only some answers to the AIDS crisis but the best answers that we can envision at the present time.

Chapter I
The Medical Perspective*

Dr. Paul O'Keefe
Chief of Infectious Disease Section,
Loyola University School of Medicine

* Excerpted from the original Conference presentation
  and adapted for this publication

Introduction and Definition

AIDS or Acquired Immunodeficiency Syndrome first appeared in the United States in 1981. At that time, a report of five young homosexual men from the Los Angeles area with pneumocystis carinii pneumonia was published. This type of pneumonia in previously healthy young men produced immediate concern to epidemiologists at the Centers for Disease Control (CDC) and resulted in the development of a case definition which the medical community could use in reporting cases to the CDC. The definition includes two components:

1. A presence of a disease process. Either an opportunistic infection or a malignant disorder, which is predictive of underlying severe immunodeficiency.
2. No other known cause for the immune deficiency such as the presence of some other malignancy or immunosuppressive therapy exists.

Opportunistic Infections

The list of opportunistic infections which are used to signify underlying immune deficiency is a long one, inclusive of:

1. Protozoan Infections: Pneumocystis carinii pneumonia is the most frequent opportunistic infection seen in patients with AIDS.
2. Fungal Infections: Candida Esophagitis (yeast infections of the esophagus) and cryptococcal meningitis are common.
3. Bacterial Infections: Tuberculosis and infections caused by related mycobacterial organisms are common.
4. Viral infections: One sees atypical manifestations of relatively common viral infections. For example, Herpes which causes infection in many normal people tends to produce a more serious problem in patients with AIDS. Instead of a small cold sore, or a small genital lesion which lasts a week or so, AIDS patients get progressive extension of the cold sore on to the face or of the genital lesions to involve large areas of the genitalia. These progressive lesions last for weeks and weeks.

Malignant Disorders

AIDS patients have been subject to certain malignant disorders. The most important is Kaposi's Sarcoma: A single or group of pigmented nodules on the skin and mucosal surfaces. Advanced forms spread to organs including the lungs and liver. The other malignancy that the patients develop is a primary brain lymphoma. Although lymphomas are common, a lymphoma which begins in and is limited to the brain is very uncommon and suggests a disorder of immunity.

Epidemiology

As of this time the CDC has accumulated over 40,000 cases of AIDS. Based on the estimated prevalence of 1.5 million individuals infected with the Human Immunodeficiency Virus (HIV), public health experts estimate that by 1991, between 220,000 and 350,000 cases of AIDS will have been reported. This will clearly have an enormous impact on health care delivery as well as all of the support systems on which the health care delivery system relies.

Most of the cases of AIDS reported so far have occurred in certain population groups. Of those cases, homosexual and bisexual men are the most common group. They account for 66% of accumulated cases. Intravenous drug abusers are the second largest group of AIDS cases. When IV drug abusers alone and IV drug abusers who are also homosexual or bisexual males are included, they account for 25% of AIDS cases. Heterosexual transmission accounts for approximately 4% of the cases. Heterosexual spread has not occurred as rapidly as public health officials estimated. Studies would suggest that heterosexual transmission does not occur with each act of sexual intercourse.

The AIDS Virus

AIDS has been shown to be caused by a virus currently known as the Human Immunodeficiency Virus. Initially, the agent was discovered in several laboratories, each of which gave a name to the virus. We heard about HTLV-III, AIDS-associated virus, and lymphadenopathy-associated virus.

The discoveries in the fields of virology and molecular biology surrounding the identification of this virus have been truly amazing. The genetic material of the virus has been carefully analyzed. Nearly all of the genes have been identified and many gene products cloned.

Of the several definitions for AIDS-Related Complex, the one which I will discuss requires that there be any two or more of the following:
1. Fatigue, diarrhea or fever greater than 37.8 C lasting two or more days within the preceding six months.
2. Unintentional weight loss of greater than 4.5kg within the preceding six months.
3. Potassium hydroxide confirmed oral candidiasis.

This definition is required for epidemiologic studies, but more generally AIDS-Related Complex refers to a group of symptoms and signs including fever, diarrhea and weight loss for which no other cause can be identified.

AIDS Testing

Current available testing for evidence of HIV infection in humans involves tests which demonstrate antibody to the HIV virus.

Elisa Test

The screening test most widely used is an Elisa test which measures antibodies to several of the antigens produced by the virus. This is a very sensitive test, being positive in more than 98% of the patients with AIDS. There can be false positive tests, however, and positive Elisa tests should be confirmed with a Western Blot test.

Western Blot

The Western Blot also measures antibodies to a number of core and envelope antigens of the virus. It can be used to monitor the progression of infection. Recently, a test has been developed to detect antigen levels in the blood by Elisa technique. A recent publication in the *Journal of the American Medical Association* demonstrated the usefulness of the antigen test in diagnosing early infection. It is not widely used currently and its place in testing for HIV virus has yet to be determined.

In looking at the number of infected individuals in the population, those with AIDS, ARC (AIDS-Related Complex), lymphadenopathy syndrome or central nervous system disease represent only the tip of the iceberg. Aside from the known cases, there is a very large number of individuals who are capable of transmitting infection but show no signs of disease.

Transmission of HIV

The most important mode of transmission of HIV is through blood and semen. Blood products which are used medically, including red blood cells, plasma, platelets and factor concentrates which are used in hemophiliac patients, are all capable of transmitting the virus. All blood products which are used medically are now tested for HIV. This has reduced the likelihood of transmission. The factor concentrates used in hemophiliacs are heat-treated, a process which inactivates the virus. It is very likely that these products are also no longer transmitting the infection. We are certain that semen can transmit the infection by the reports of transmission of AIDS to women recipients of human semen in the process of artificial insemination. The virus has also been isolated from saliva, tears, breast milk and urine. None of these have been definitively shown to transmit the virus and it is highly likely that they do not. One study looking at the likelihood of recovering virus from saliva of patients who are seropositive for HIV showed that the virus was recovered from 28 of 50 blood samples from this group of patients but from only 1 out of 83 samples of saliva. Other studies have shown that when virus is present in saliva the amount is very low in comparison to that which is present in blood. Thus, it is very unlikely that the infection will be transmitted by contact with saliva only.

There are four routes of transmission:

1. Sexual transmission occurs in homosexual activity between men, particularly when receptive anal intercourse is practiced.
2. Heterosexual transmission occurs both from men to women and from women to men. It is still not certain what the likelihood of transmission from a single heterosexual contact is.
3. Exposure to blood, including blood transfusions and sharing of needles and syringes by intravenous drug abusers, is an important means of transmission.
4. Prenatal transmission from an infected mother to her infant occurs with high frequency. The majority of these infected neonates develop AIDS.

To prevent sexual transmission of HIV infection the safest recommendation is to refrain from having sex or to maintain a monogamous sexual relationship with a partner who is either known to test negative or with whom the mutually faithful monogamous relationship has been going on since before 1978. Obviously sex with members of known risk groups increases the likelihood of acquiring infection. Increasing numbers of sex partners also heightens the risk. Finally, condoms should decrease the likelihood of transmission if they are properly used. Up to this point, well-done studies proving the efficacy of condoms have not been published. One small study done on prostitutes from Zaire disclosed that only one of six prostitutes who insisted on use of condoms by 75% or more of their customers was seropositive. Whereas in 298 prostitutes who did not insist on use of condoms by their customers, 74 or 26% were seropositive. This is not a perfect study but does suggest that there may be some protection if condoms are used consistently.

To prevent transmission by IV drug abusers it is recommended that they stop using IV drugs if at all possible. If they continue to use drugs, needles and other IV drug abuse paraphernalia must not be shared.

I would recommend that you all read the Surgeon General's report. In it he clearly states the known scientific facts about transmission of the AIDS virus. It is a very well written document which contains much useful information. Dr. Koop also makes recommendations to the general population about the prevention of AIDS which are very straightforward and to the point.

Treatment

A number of agents have been tried in an effort to treat patients with AIDS. The interferons; suramin, an antiparasitic drug used for many years in the treatment of African Trypanosomiasis or sleeping sickness; antimoniotungstate, agent similar to suramin; and trisodiumphosphonoformate have all been proven ineffective in clinical trials. Ribavirin, a drug which interferes with RNA synthesis in viruses, is currently undergoing trials. Azidothymidine, or AZT, has been shown effective in clinical trials and is now available for general use. The trials compared AZT in 145 patients with AIDS who had recovered from an episode of pneumocystis carinii pneumonia with placebo in 137 similarly chosen patients. At the time of analysis there was one death in the AZT group compared with 16 in the placebo group and 36 AIDS-related events in the AZT group compared with 59 in the placebo group. At this time the code was broken and because it was considered unethical no more placebo-controlled trials with AZT were carried out. AZT had significant side effects, including bone marrow toxicity resulting in anemia and requiring blood transfusions in a substantial number of patients and leukopenia or low white blood count. There are a number of other drugs with activities similar to AZT which hold promise and are undergoing clinical trials presently. Also, novel agents including Peptide T, a synthetic peptide neurotransmitter which interacts with the T-4 receptor, were discovered by workers at the National Institutes of Mental Health and are undergoing clinical trials.

Development of an effective AIDS vaccine is somewhat less promising. Nearly all of the protein gene products of the HIV have been cloned or synthesized. Several of these have been shown to induce antibodies in animals but so far that antibody response has not been protective. Some preliminary work in humans by French workers was reported at the National AIDS Conference in Washington a few months ago.

Casual and Workplace Transmission

Studies have been done in situations in which transmission would be anticipated to be likely, namely, household contacts of patients with AIDS and health care workers. About half a dozen studies have been published on household contacts. The most widely quoted is the so-called Friedland study done in New York City. This study looked at 101 household contacts of persons with AIDS. These contacts were frequently parents or siblings who were closely involved with the care of these sick and sometimes dying individuals. All were tested for evidence of HIV infection, and the infection was found in only one, an under-six-year-old biologic offspring of a patient with AIDS in whom perinatal transmission was most probable. None of the other studies have shown any evidence of AIDS in household contacts. Single reports have been published which appear to document transmission in this setting, one report of transmission to a brother from a patient with AIDS and the other to a nurse in England who was caring for a patient with AIDS in the home setting. Despite these reports, the best epidemiological evidence suggests that transmission in the home setting does not occur unless the contacts are biologic offspring, sex partners or needle sharers.

Studies in health care workers done by the Centers for Disease Control and others have suggested that transmission in this setting is also very unlikely. Again, the best studies involve needle-sticks or accidental exposure of mucous membranes such as the lining of the mouth or the eye to blood or other potentially infected body fluids of patients with AIDS. Of 451 such exposures documented by the CDC, only two of the contacts were seropositive. One of these showed definite evidence of seroconversion.

Precautions

After these reports we were very complacent about the nonlikelihood of transmission as a result of home or health care setting contact. The evidence clearly states that AIDS is not transmitted by casual contact. However, in May of 1987, a report of transmission of the virus to three health care workers who had brief or trivial contact with blood did bring about a change in the recommendations for prevention of AIDS in the health care setting. Up until that time patients with AIDS or HIV infection were placed in blood and body fluid precautions when they were admitted to the hospital. This entailed placing a sign on the door of the room indicating the type of precautions and recommending that health care personnel wear gloves, eye protection, and mouth and nose protection should an exposure to blood or bodily fluids be anticipated. Therefore, when drawing blood or starting intravenous lines, gloves were worn. Eyecovering and masks were worn for procedures which might result in splashing of blood or infected fluids into the eyes or mouth.

After the report of the three health care workers, the CDC recommended universal precautions. This change in recommendations was suggested because the identification of infected patients, although protecting health care workers in that setting, did nothing to protect health care workers from individuals who were infected but who were not known to be positive. It is estimated that there are just as many and probably more such infected patients admitted to hospitals.

Universal precautions require that health care workers treat all patients as if they are potentially infectious and therefore use gloves, eyecovering, and mask if there is any anticipated exposure to blood or body fluids.

I believe that these recommendations for universal precautions should be carried over to non-hospital settings when anticipated exposure to blood or body fluids is likely to occur. Specifically ambulance crews and paramedics should practice the same universal precautions in the field that health care workers practice in the hospital. A recent study looking at unsuspected HIV infection in emergency room patients done at the Johns Hopkins Hospital in Baltimore disclosed that 3% of all emergency room patients, 6% of trauma patients and 16% of trauma patients between the ages of 25 and 34 were infected with the virus. We do not know whether this level of seropositivity is present in Chicago or other parts of the country, but it is inevitable that some emergency room patients will be infected. I therefore feel strongly that the CDC recommendations for universal precautions should be followed by all personnel who are involved in the care and transportation of sick people or trauma victims both within and outside the hospital.

Casual and workplace transmission is very unlikely but by practicing universal precautions, workers involved in the care of sick patients or trauma victims both within and outside the hospital can protect themselves from infection with HIV.

Chapter II
The National Perspective on Research and Policy Issues

Theodore Hammett
Associate, Abt Associates

AIDS Cases Among Correctional Inmates

In the fall of 1985, we found a total of 766 inmate cases of AIDS in correctional institutions in the United States. This included the Federal Bureau of Prisons, all fifty state correctional systems and thirty-three large city and county jail systems. By the fall of 1986, about a year later, that number had increased from 766 to 1232 – an increase of 61%. This is a sharp increase to be sure, but it is not as sharp an increase as was experienced during the same time period in the general population of the U.S. – almost 80%.

The vast majority of inmate cases, according to the correctional systems, were associated with IV drug abuse. As of the fall of 1986, there had been 529 deaths from AIDS among correctional inmates while in custody. About half of these occurred between 1985 and 1986.

The important thing to know about these numbers is that these cases were by no means evenly distributed across the country. There is a highly uneven distribution across correctional systems and across geographical regions. The vast majority of correctional systems, even in 1986, had very few or no cases of AIDS among their inmates and only a very small number of correctional systems had any significant number of AIDS cases among their inmates. The correctional systems that had the large number of cases were concentrated in the middle Atlantic states, primarily The New York State Department of Correctional Services, The New Jersey Department of Corrections and The New York City Department of Corrections. Elsewhere in the country, systems with relatively significant numbers of cases were in Florida, Texas and California. The distribution is very unevenly weighted toward the middle Atlantic region of the country and we expect it to continue this way for the foreseeable future, although it is important to point out that as time goes on more and more correctional systems will experience at least one case of AIDS among their inmates.

The uneven distribution reflects the prevalence of infection among IV drug-using populations in the United States. The rate of HIV infection among IV drug users is much higher in the New York City metropolitan area and northern New Jersey, for example, than it is anywhere else in the country. This accounts for the large numbers of AIDS cases found in the New York State, New York City and New Jersey State correctional systems. It is estimated now that possibly 60%-70% of all IV drug abusers in the New York City metropolitan area are infected with HIV. These numbers are by far the highest that we know of in the country. Even if you look as close as southern New Jersey, you find much lower rates of infection among IV drug users – about 5%-10%. Available information for Chicago suggests that the rate is also about 5%-10%. Other areas of the country have varying rates of infection among IV drug abusers: Miami – 25%; San Francisco and Los Angeles – 5%-15%.

This wide variation in infection rates among IV drug users outside correctional facilities is what we are seeing translated into AIDS cases in the correctional systems.

There have been no job-related cases of AIDS or HIV infection among any of the following categories of workers to date:

1. correctional staff
2. police officers
3. probation or parole officers
4. court officers
5. emergency medical technicians or other public safety workers

There have been cases of AIDS among correctional officers in certain jurisdictions but these have been related to independent risk factors – that is, risk factors in these individuals' private lives.

Education and Training

Education and training must be the cornerstone of the law enforcement response to AIDS, as it should be the cornerstone of everyone's response to AIDS. At this point we do not have effective treatments or vaccines for this infection. Law enforcement and criminal justice agencies must use education and training to overcome fear resulting from misinformation about AIDS or the fear may severely affect the operational effectiveness of these agencies and affect the quality of service delivered by these agencies.

It is important that criminal justice agencies develop and implement training at the earliest possible moment and not rely upon the mass media as a source of information for their staff. In fact, our survey of police departments revealed that the mass media were the source of most of the concern and misinformation about AIDS. Therefore, it is important to provide your own education and training to get the facts out and let people know regularly what the truth is so that they can go about their duties in an effective manner.

Armed with accurate information about AIDS, law enforcement and criminal justice professionals can act as educators in the community. They can help the people they come in contact with on a daily basis learn about AIDS and how to cope with AIDS. Law enforcement officers, of any group of workers in our society, probably come into more frequent and regular contact with members of AIDS risk groups – particularly IV drug users and prostitutes. AIDS is a matter to be concerned about, and to take precautionary measures against. It also represents an opportunity for criminal justice and law enforcement personnel to become educators in their own communities and to help the community at large to cope with this very serious problem.

Overall, law enforcement and criminal justice agencies that invest in high-quality training and education – and it is expensive –

invest not only in the welfare of their own staff, but also in the welfare, ultimately, of the community at large.

Principles of High-Quality Education and Training on AIDS

1. **Education should be timely.** It should be begun, if possible, before widespread fear and misinformation have a chance to appear. It may be too late for this in many instances but this is the best approach.

2. **Training must be presented on a regular basis.** Since there is new information, or supposedly new information, about this disease coming out all the time, it is important that updates be presented. Agencies should assign someone to keep abreast of the information and to prepare timely updates; concerns can then be addressed as they appear. A classic example of this is the case of the three health care workers reported by CDC in May 1987 to have been infected with HIV through non-needle-stick exposures to blood. Many categories of workers – including health care and public safety workers – were extremely concerned about this report. The press coverage seemed to suggest that these cases represented "new information" that more superficial exposures would result in infection. In fact, all three of the infected health care workers had experienced blood-to-open-wound or blood-to-mucous-membrane rare exposures, which have long been known to be possible means of transmission. Moreover, all three workers were in violation of CDC-recommended infection control procedures at the time of the incidents which resulted in their infection. This information should have been promptly presented to concerned employees in every workplace.

3. **Training needs to be live.** It is not enough to bring people into a room, show them a videotape, and usher them out. You must have knowledgeable people come in, present information, and be available to answer questions, so that people can raise their specific concerns and get answers from people who have substantive expertise.

4. **Education and training must be keyed to specific law enforcement situations and concerns.** Again, it is not enough to show a generic videotape, or distribute a generic brochure about AIDS. Specific concerns and issues occur to criminal justice, law enforcement and corrections professionals and these need to be addressed very specifically in the training. Some of the key subjects that ought to be included in a training program include: means of transmission, precautionary measures, procedures for CPR and first aid, search procedures, arrest procedures, and transportation procedures. In our document on *AIDS and the Law Enforcement Officer* you will find all of these

subjects detailed – crime scene procedures, evidence handling procedures, disposal of contaminated materials, lockup procedures, body removal procedures, and so forth. All of these are specific areas of concern to law enforcement and criminal justice and need to be addressed in training and educational programs.

5. **The tone of education and training needs to strike a very careful balance, avoiding the extremes of alarmism and complacency.** In other words, we must state forthrightly that this is a serious problem. But we do not want to create hysteria through our education and training. We do not want to fuel fear based on misinformation nor do we, at the other extreme, want to lull people into a false sense of security. We want people to understand that this is a serious disease but that it is only transmitted by a certain few, well-defined means.

Our education and training efforts ought to focus on ways to prevent transmission by those certain few, well-defined means. It is a difficult balance to strike, because if you raise the issue you contribute to concern. There is, however, a level of reasonable and rational concern which needs to be approached and reached but beyond which it is harmful to go.

Important Educational Messages

What are some examples of educational messages that should be presented to criminal justice and law enforcement? These educational messages represent an attempt to formulate a rational and consistent approach appropriate to the real level of risk involved.

Human Bites

This concern is often raised by corrections, law enforcement and criminal justice professionals. There is strong scientific evidence as to the extremely low concentrations of the virus found in saliva and the extremely low risk of transmission through saliva. There have been no documented cases of transmission of the virus through saliva. Presenting this evidence is one part of responding to concerns about human bites. The other is the importance of pointing out the mechanics of a human bite: in order for the virus to be transmitted through blood in a human bite, the infected person who bites someone else must have his/her own blood in his/her mouth, and break the skin of the victim in order to transmit that blood into the blood stream of the victim. If you think of it in these terms, it is not a very likely scenario to occur. Simply transmitting saliva into an open wound is very unlikely to transmit the virus. The only way that it is likely to happen is for the blood of the person doing the biting to get into the blood of the person who is bitten.

Even if this occurs, there are some precautionary measures that can be taken after such an event. It should be handled in the same manner as a snake bite; that is, the wound should be "milked" so that it begins to bleed. Thus, any infected blood will probably be discharged from the wound. Then that area ought to be carefully washed with hot water and soap and medical attention should be sought immediately.

Spitting Incidents

Spitting incidents represent another area of concern to criminal justice and law enforcement. Here again, the evidence regarding saliva should be presented.

Urine and Other Body Fluids

Another area of concern is the possibility of being splashed with urine or other body fluids. These body fluids have been found to contain an extremely low concentration of the virus. In order to be infected through urine or saliva, you would have to have approximately one quart of the fluid enter your blood stream. There is an extremely low probability of this happening. If someone dumped a quart bucket of urine over your head, it would not be a very pleasant experience, but it would not be enough to transmit the infection. That quart of fluid would have to enter your blood stream in order for infection to occur.

Dried Blood

Another issue which has been of some concern to criminal justice staff is the presence of dried blood at crime scenes or elsewhere. An article published in the *Journal of the American Medical Association* last spring reported on a laboratory study using preparations of HIV 100,000 times as concentrated as would be found in a normal blood sample. This study was undertaken to test the effectiveness of laboratory precautionary procedures; it was not intended to show what would happen with blood samples in the real world. This study found that there was detectable virus after three days in highly concentrated viral preparations which had dried. However, in normal blood samples, the drying process itself inactivates the virus. No detectable virus can be found in a dried sample of normal human blood. It can only be found in highly concentrated viral preparations created in the laboratory.

There have been suggestions that if a dried blood sample is rehydrated, the virus comes back to life. This is simply not true. Once the virus is dead, it is permanently dead.

Reasonable and Consistent Precautionary Measures

In the past six months to one year, more and more criminal justice and corrections agencies have developed and promulgated comprehensive policies on AIDS. This is a good thing. There is a need to clarify policies and to establish procedures that can be enforced and monitored. There is also a need for consistently applied policies. This is the most important part of all. In the wake of the infection of the three health care workers mentioned earlier, CDC has now recommended universal precautions in health care; this means treating all patients as if they are infected with HIV by avoiding all unprotected contact with their blood or other body fluids.

This ought to be done in all public safety employments as well. It is not necessary to know whether a person is HIV seropositive or not; everyone should be assumed to be infected when it comes to dealing with blood or body fluids. In fact, even before AIDS became an issue, it was never a good idea to have unprotected contact with the blood or body fluids of anyone. Hepatitis-B and other diseases can also be transmitted through blood and body fluids and these are important to avoid as well. So if there is a silver lining to this issue it may be that it is causing a resurgence of concern for the application of normal, good sense hygiene procedures in a wide range of situations.

Procedures for Contact with Blood or Body Fluids

What should be done if contact with blood or body fluids is anticipated or occurs? Gloves should be worn. In addition, a protective, self-help barrier that can be set up in advance is to cover all open wounds and breaks in the skin so that you do not provide avenues of entrance for the virus. Any spills of blood or body fluids should be cleaned up promptly with a solution of water and household bleach. Following any contact, individuals involved should wash thoroughly with hot water and soap.

CPR Procedures

One-way airways for the administration of CPR are now available. This prevents the saliva or vomitus of the victim from entering the mouth of the caregiver. These should always be used when providing CPR.

Search Procedures

Correctional officers, police officers and others who may have occasion to conduct searches should require the subject to empty his/her own pockets, if possible. There are now special mirrors available that can be used to search areas so that you do not have to reach in without being able to see. Gloves should be worn for searches. Obviously, gloves cannot completely eliminate the possibility of a puncture by a needle or sharp object. The only kind of glove that can do that would be a glove that would make it impossible to conduct the search. Rubber gloves or surgical gloves will not prevent the puncture from occurring, but if they are used in conjunction with slow and careful movement in the area, they will significantly reduce the possibility of any needle-sticks or punctures.

Training, education, and precautionary measures have proven to be effective in criminal justice and law enforcement settings. It is important to embody these precautionary measures in your policies, education and training, and to take strong steps to insure that they are implemented in a very consistent and professional way.

HIV Antibody Testing

I will discuss HIV antibody testing briefly in three contexts: first, with regard to correctional inmates; second, with regard to probation, parole and community corrections; and third, with regard to incidents which may occur involving citizens and criminal justice professionals.

Testing of Correctional Inmates

In the correctional context, testing is a highly controversial subject now and one that has become, in the past few months, highly politicized. The president, attorney general and American Medical Association all recommend that the Federal Bureau of Prisons begin testing all correctional inmates for AIDS.

In Illinois the legislature passed a law which would have required mandatory testing of all inmates of the Illinois Department of Corrections, but the governor vetoed that particular part of the legislative package. This is a situation which is changing rapidly. As of now, we know of about ten states, in addition to the Federal Bureau of Prisons, which are testing all of their inmates.

The most common argument in favor of testing is that it is a way of learning the extent of the problem, of making informed budget and facilities planning decisions, and of targeting education and prevention programs. I think there are some difficulties with these arguments. One is that you can learn the extent of the problem by doing blind epidemiological studies. You do not need to link test results with individuals. In fact, a study of this kind is about to begin in the Illinois Department of Corrections.

As far as targeting education and prevention is concerned, it is important to decide in advance exactly what you are going to do with the test results before you embark upon a program of mass testing in a correctional population. Without knowing that, and without deciding what good this information is going to do you in very specific terms, it is not a worthwhile thing to do. In fact, it could have very detrimental effects.

There are a number of arguments against mass HIV antibody screening in correctional institutions. One is the test itself. There are some serious problems with false positives and false negatives on the test. In particular, it has been suggested by some investigators that IV drug users may be particularly prone to false positives, and since IV drug users make up large percentages of correctional populations, this could be a problem. There is the problem of the lag time of three to twelve weeks between infection and appearance of the antibodies. Recent data suggests that this lag time can be as long as eighteen months in a significant minority of cases. Again, the test does not detect the virus itself; it detects antibodies to the virus and during the lag time between infection and appearance of the antibodies, a person is actually infected and able to infect others but will not test positive. This presents some real logistical problems, in terms of implementing a testing program in a correctional environment or anywhere else, because it is going to be impossible through one wave of testing to identify all of the infected people. It will be necessary to do repeated follow-up testing in order to have any hope of capturing the population of interest.

There are high costs associated with testing. In addition, there are serious problems with confidentiality, particularly in a correctional environment where rumors spread rapidly – both true and false rumors – and where there may be intimidation and violence against people, either believed or known to be seropositive. There may also be a range of types of discrimination after the person is released.

Another important argument is that testing can really undermine the aims of an educational program. It can create a false sense of security in a population by saying, on this side are the people you have to be worried about and on the other side are the people you do not have to worry about. That is a very dangerous message to send. The fact is that everyone needs to be worried about certain specific behaviors. You cannot categorize people and be sure that you have reduced your risk.

A final argument against testing is that the limited data available so far suggests that there has not been very much transmission of the virus among correctional inmates. If this changes it might suggest a reconsideration of the whole issue but, as of now, the evidence suggests there is not a great deal of transmission occurring.

Testing in Probation and Parole

The major issue for probation and parole is not mass screening – this is unlikely to occur. Rather, the key concern is the extent of the officers' responsibility to notify spouses, sexual partners, employers, or residential placement supervisors of clients they learn are infected with HIV. CDC has recently issued recommendations for health care professionals dealing with the difficult situation in which a seropositive person is counseled to notify his sexual partners but refuses to do so. CDC now recommends that the health care workers, and possibly by analogy the probation or parole officers, take confidential steps to make that notification themselves. This is a very sensitive and difficult area but it is one in which there are obviously very high stakes and one in which there are very serious moral, as well as civil liberty, questions.

Testing in Response to Incidents

A third context in which testing should be considered is when an incident occurs involving a suspect or subject and a member of a criminal justice or law enforcement agency. Again, applicable state laws need to be taken into consideration. Many states have laws which prohibit the testing of anyone without his/her informed consent. This is an area which can cause some serious problems if a police officer, probation officer or correctional officer believes that he or she may have been infected through an incident and wants to find out whether or not the other individual involved is seropositive. Under current law it may be impossible to require that person to be tested. Of course it is certainly possible for the officer involved to be tested and to take action accordingly. There was recently a case in Massachusetts involving an incident in which an inmate allegedly scratched and spat on a correctional officer. The officer sought a court order requiring the inmate to be tested but the judge declined to issue the order on two grounds: first, because any involuntary testing is prohibited by state law; and second, because scientific evidence strongly indicates that the risk of transmission occurring as a result of such an incident is extremely remote.

Chapter III
The Legal Perspective

Harvey Grossman
Legal Director, ACLU of Illinois

AIDS is not a civil liberties problem. AIDS is not a public health problem. AIDS is our problem. The message is that we must repudiate an "us versus them" approach and accept AIDS as being a problem for all of society.

First, I will address a false issue – that within the AIDS crisis there is a tension between protecting civil liberties and also serving the public health. To a great extent, that tension does not exist at all. In fact, measures that effectively protect the public health in this crisis also respect individual rights. Voluntary noncoercive approaches are the answer in dealing with AIDS. Punitive, coercive measures will drive the disease underground and will force those people who are at greatest risk away from centers of knowledge and counseling. Potentially, this will lead them, in their ignorance, to spread the disease and actually threaten the public health.

The second point that I seek to make is that it is important to extend and enforce antidiscrimination laws and basic constitutional protections for persons with AIDS and those who are at increased risk of AIDS. Again, the message is that in so doing, we ultimately protect the public health in addition to protecting those values of individual freedom which are important to our society.

Finally, I hope to convey that people in law enforcement and corrections have special obligations in this epidemic. Because they are decision- and policy-makers in our society and because in many instances they control the most direct exercise of government power on the street, it is critical that they examine their profession's own performance and seek to impose normative standards on members of their profession. While certain behaviors and practices may be lawful, they may nevertheless harm the public good by increasing unwarranted fears in our community and reinforcing behavior that may again ultimately harm the public health.

In order to insure an understanding of my comments, I would like to re-establish some of the basic scientific facts about AIDS. First, at this point, we have no cure for AIDS. There is the availability of limited treatment and that availability is well known to persons with AIDS and those who are at increased risk of AIDS. AIDS is spread by voluntary behavior: through the exchange of blood products; by semen and vaginal secretions during sex; by contaminated needles through IV drug use; and by an infected mother to her fetus or infant. We know that at present education is the only answer. Testing itself may not reinforce the lesson we can provide through counseling and education. But we do know now that education is effective. For example, a recent and reliable scientific study showed a decrease in the rate of infection in the high-risk communities of bisexual and homosexual men in Chicago without mandatory testing.

Beyond the scientific facts, in order to understand AIDS and our response to AIDS, it is critical that we identify the issues we will encounter. We must address homosexuality, illicit drug use and death. These are issues that many people have never had to confront directly. In dealing with homosexual and bisexual men we are presented with behaviors that some in society find offensive and indeed, some states make illegal. In dealing with drug use, we are exposed to a subculture that is foreign to many of us. But we must understand that subculture. The IV drug-using population presents the greatest threat of a tertiary spread of this disease in our society today. Not addressing that problem or penalizing that community with a lack of supportive services will do no more than increase the risk to the rest of society.

We also must consider death and confront our own sense of death and dying. Our fear of death, or our fear of our own death, may cause us to shun people with terminal illness. This is particularly true of people who have AIDS because some people find it easy to blame the AIDS victim. This fear also makes us tolerate public policy and behavior by public officials that ultimately will be harmful to society.

The discrimination in our society toward people with AIDS and those who are at risk of getting AIDS or are perceived as having AIDS is absolutely overwhelming. For the last eighteen months two lawyers in my office, including myself, have been inundated with a volume of discrimination complaints. From the individual clients and the kinds of injury and suffering that I see every day in my practice, it is apparent that AIDS has an impact on people of all colors, genders, ages, sexual orientations and economic and social classes. The people are us. The problem is ours.

There are two ways the government can approach this problem. The first way is through a coercive or compulsive approach. That type of model involves: forced testing; mandatory reporting of a person's antibody status; contact tracing under penalty of criminal sanction for needle contacts and sexual contacts; forced treatment – quarantine and isolation; and finally, criminal sanctions. Indeed, we are now seeing forced testing in the Federal Bureau of Prisons and the proposal has surfaced in many states around the country. I think the governor in Illinois was prudent to veto such a measure in this state.

The voluntary model, on the other hand, is based on the ability to educate people; to fund supportive services; to eradicate stigma; and not to generate and reinforce hysteria in our society. In particular, it is based on the premise that public policy action should not be taken on the likelihood of rare occurrences and remote risks.

There is an additional overlay to these models and that is the restraint that can be imposed by law should government resort to overly coercive approaches to the AIDS epidemic. There are some very old court decisions in this country concerning public health. That early law broadly defined what are called the police powers of the state – the power of the state to act for the benefit of the health and welfare of society in general. There presently are policy-makers who rely on those early court decisions in trying to legitimize the coercive or compulsive model of resolving problems arising from the epidemic.

I believe that the early law is antiquated and has lost its vitality. There is, however, a more recent and well-developed body of law, beginning in the 1960's, that recognizes the individual rights of persons with disabilities. Some of those cases have even involved persons with contagious diseases. Specifically, a case brought by the American Civil Liberties Union during the 1970's to protect children with Hepatitis-B Virus in the public school system resulted in establishing a basic precedent which is applicable to people with AIDS. Subsequent cases have established that persons with contagious diseases and AIDS specifically will be recognized as having a "handicap" under federal handicap discrimination law. The federal law is applicable to programs that receive federal financial assistance and protects "handicapped" persons in all aspects of association with the program (e.g., employment or participation as a recipient of services of benefits). Many local and state law enforcement and corrections agencies are covered by this federal law because they receive federal dollars.

In addition, other handicap discrimination laws are in place in many states and localities around the country. In fact, over 35 jurisdictions have recognized that AIDS is a "handicap" for purposes of their own state and local antidiscrimination laws. These laws generally protect the rights of persons with AIDS, or persons who are perceived as having AIDS, against private persons in places of public accommodation, in employment and in housing.

In the AIDS context all of the handicap discrimination laws basically require that no discriminatory action be taken unless there is a real and significant risk of harm posed by the presence or action of the person with AIDS (or HIV infection).

In regard to the workplace setting the relevant guidelines were issued by the Centers for Disease Control in November of 1985. If you violate those guidelines, you will most likely violate the legal norms and you are likely to find yourself the subject of state or federal antidiscrimination litigation. An important principle in the employment context is that future inability to perform the job due to a handicap is not a basis for termination of an employee or refusal to hire an employee. It is present ability to perform that is the legal index. When someone is antibody-positive, you do not have an indication from that status that they will not be able to perform at the present time. Indeed, you know very little about future performance. The likelihood of developing symptoms of AIDS after HIV infection increases with time, but the data on that point is not clear yet. We do know that people two years, five years, even seven years after initial infection are still asymptomatic.

In addition, a refusal to hire someone who is HIV-positive, based on some notion of increased cost of fringe benefits or insurance or other potential future increased costs, is not a legitimate basis for discrimination. Also, refusal to work with people who have HIV infection is unlawful. You can take action against persons or co-employees who refuse to work in those circumstances and your position will be sustained in the courts. Employees who threaten a walk-out unless you remove an employee with HIV infection from the workforce will violate the National Labor Relations Act because there is not a "reasonable" threat to their health by working along-side a person with HIV infection. But you as employers can insure against that walk-out by providing good education at the workplace and not waiting for the first case of HIV infection among employees before your workforce is educated.

In addition to antidiscrimination laws, there is basic constitutional protection of privacy and liberty and from government taking action on the basis of unwarranted, generalized fears or remote risks. That principle has been very recently affirmed by the United States Supreme Court in a case which struck down a zoning law when a municipality sought to prevent persons with developmental disabilities from having group homes in their own community. The municipality argued that adult mentally retarded people pose a potential threat or harm to the community; but the Supreme Court responded quite strongly that undifferentiated fears could not be a basis for discriminating against and segregating those people in our society.

In terms of law enforcement and corrections, you will be interacting in your communities with people who have AIDS or are perceived as having AIDS and who also have basic constitutional and statutory protections from discrimination at the hands of law enforcement and corrections agencies. In those instances where you do not act on the basis of documented, significant risks of harm, as opposed to undifferentiated or generalized fears, you risk violating the law.

Constitutional protections also extend to protecting private medical information of persons who are employees of government and persons who receive services from government population. The Supreme Court has held that we all have a constitutional right of privacy in personal medical information unless government can show a legitimate need for that information. Curiosity is not a legitimate need for information. Someone's HIV status is not something that very many agencies of government have a legitimate need to know. Somebody's antibody status alone may not ever be a legitimate objective for government. Indeed, in this state, Dr. Turnock, the Director of the Illinois Department of Public Health, has publicly stated that his agency has no need for the names of persons who merely test positive for the presence of the antibody.

I suggest, on the basis of the law which I have reviewed, some guidelines for policy-making. Before government adopts any measures which would infringe upon the individual civil liberties of people with AIDS and those perceived as having AIDS, those actions or measures must meet the following criteria:

1. The measure must be based on the most current and comprehensive scientific and medical information.
2. The measure must be carefully tailored and not be overboard.
3. The measure should minimize any adverse impact on privacy, on equality and other fundamental rights.
4. There must be no feasible alternative that is less restrictive on individual rights that would accomplish government's legitimate objective.

The last point is the statement of a legal doctrine referred to as "the least restrictive alternative." If policy-makers keep that concept in mind before they take action they should be able to protect government's legitimate interest and still act in a manner that respects the individual. An important point is that the doctrine does not require government to be ineffective. In order to apply the doctrine we consider only that which is effective. If there are two approaches which are equally effective, we must take the one that is least restrictive of individual rights. But if the least restrictive alternative is not equally effective, one need not resort to it.

Finally, my third point is that those within law enforcement and corrections have a responsibility to police themselves – not just through laws or regulations but through peer pressure – by condemning those professionals who act in a manner that while lawful, nevertheless results in reinforcing unwarranted fears and hysteria in our society and shunning people with HIV infection. An example of such conduct at the street enforcement level is the wearing of gloves when policing a demonstration in support of gay and lesbian rights. I am using similar facts in a lawsuit to show intentional discrimination on the part of law enforcement in making an unlawful raid on a gay bar here in Chicago. In that particular instance, all of the agents who participated in the raid put on gloves before they did pat-down searches of over fifty patrons of a bar. I have a separate claim in that lawsuit which seeks redress for intentional discrimination under the 14th Amendment based on discrimination based on sexual orientation.

The use of the gloves, as in this example, will have at least two negative consequences.

1. The media will cover that conduct because it is "news." I do not chastise the media for doing their job, but, if unaccompanied by some editorial comment, the image will reinforce the unwarranted fear in our community that simply coming into physical contact with a person who may be at increased risk for HIV

infection has the potential to transmit the virus.

2. In addition to that, such conduct polarizes law enforcement from a necessary and important part of our community in coping with the AIDS epidemic. It creates and perpetuates the "us versus them" model. It will be an impediment to law enforcement's relationship with that community long after we hopefully have dealt with the AIDS epidemic. While the behavior in this example is probably not unlawful, I think law enforcement should condemn those actions because they are harmful to the community and to law enforcement's image.

Prosecutors who file criminal charges for attempted murder and other variations of unlawful homicide because someone with HIV infection spits on another person also engage in conduct which, while not unlawful or violative of the code of professional responsibility for lawyers, similarly does a disservice to our community. It harms the public health as well as reinforces the notion that AIDS can be spread through saliva. While the HIV virus has been cultured or identified in saliva, saliva has never been identified as a medium of transmission of the virus in any documented case. By filing those charges which are covered by the media, prosecutors reinforce unwarranted fear. I think we, as attorneys, need to condemn the actions of prosecutors who grab the public limelight with those kinds of prosecutions.

Finally, I think treating prisoners in correctional settings, prisons and jails in a manner that makes them guinea pigs for our epidemiological survey similarly alienates law enforcement and corrections from society and misses the proper allocation of our resources. It stigmatizes people with HIV infection to segregate them in a penal setting with no benefit whatsoever to the correctional facility itself. Indeed, there are seasoned, correctional medical staffers who believe that the ultimate outcome of segregating HIV-positive people in a correctional setting will be to designate the general population as a "safe" target for sexual violence.

I have tried to convey three points which underscore the thesis that the AIDS problem is "our" problem and that we must repudiate the "us versus them" model. We must also reject the notion that there is a conspiracy among public health and medical officials in America today to deprive us of the real information. What Dr. O'Keefe, Dr. Turnock, the Centers for Disease Control and Surgeon General Koop have told us is the truth. We must depend and rely upon such people and agencies to assess the risk for us and our society. However, all of us, as members of society, as policy-makers, as law enforcement and corrections professionals, must take the responsibility ourselves to formulate the response. Our response can either reflect our humanity or defeat it.

Chapter IV
The Police Perspective

Rudolph Nimocks
Deputy Superintendent
Bureau of Administrative Services
Chicago Police Department

Generally speaking, all the things that have been recommended in this conference regarding education and training have already been adopted by the Chicago Police Department.

A training program for the Chicago Police Department has been instituted with the cooperation of Northwestern University's Medical School. The training program is conducted in a seminar room; information on AIDS is provided and personnel are encouraged to ask questions and raise their concerns. The program was initiated first for employees who had the most exposure to people who might have AIDS: lockup personnel, tactical and vice officers, and squadron officers and their supervisors. Up to the present time, approximately 1500 people have been trained. The plan calls for training of the entire police department. That is one of the best steps that an organization can take.

Police officers would like to be assured that there is no risk. This kind of absolute assurance, of course, cannot be given. An effort is being made to make available as much information as possible and to provide as many opinions as possible. The problem that is faced by the police at the present time is more psychological than medical. This is a serious problem because it can affect the performance of the individual police officer. For instance, there have been several incidents in Chicago where police officers were reluctant to perform their duties because of their fear of AIDS.

In one such incident, officers in a squadron refused to place a person on a stretcher and do other things they are ordinarily required to do because of rumors that the person was infected with AIDS. In another incident, prostitutes spit on police officers to deter them from performing their duty. Still, the department's policy is to make it very clear to all police officers that they have an obligation to carry out their responsibilities. This policy is based on the fact that police officers performing their ordinary duties are unlikely to become infected with AIDS from casual contact. The bottom line for law enforcement officers is that there are no documented cases where line police officers have contracted AIDS in the ordinary performance of their duties. This is not to say that there are no police officers who have contracted AIDS, but they got the disease through other social circumstances. In this regard, there have been one or two such cases in the Chicago Police Department.

The Chicago Police Department's first General Order addressing AIDS was issued in 1985. The most recent General Order, published last month (September, 1987), provides department members with information on procedures for handling persons with communicable diseases.

The department has provided each district as well as the Central Detention Section with a sufficient quantity of disposable gloves. For example, vehicles assigned to the various districts are now equipped with four pairs of disposable gloves which are maintained in an envelope inside the vehicle's glove compartment. These gloves are to be worn primarily when there is a possibility of contact with bodily fluids and when there is physical contact with persons who may be sick, injured or deceased, have open sores, rashes, or other visible skin disorders.

The department has also recommended some preventive measures for police officers. Thorough washing with soap and water is an important measure in preventing the spread of infectious disease and should be done to cleanse any area of the body which has come in contact with bodily fluids. Hand washing is recommended even if gloves have been worn.

The department's response to the AIDS problem must be a reasoned and prudent multi-agency approach involving public health agencies, the medical community, state and federal legislatures, and the legal community. The department's response must also consider the needs and concerns of its employees while insuring that the rights of people who have contracted AIDS are respected.

Chapter V
Panel Discussion

Law Enforcement and AIDS:
Questions of Justice and Care

Moderator: Rev. George P. Winchester, S.J.
Panelists: Dr. John A. Raba
                   JoAnne Ross
                   Caryn Berman
                   Theodore Hammett
Highlights of Questions and Answers

Rev. George P. Winchester, S.J.
Director of University Ministry
Loyola University of Chicago

The purpose of my being involved in this conference is twofold: first, I serve as the panel moderator; second, as a Roman Catholic priest I am here to assure you that not all church people are phobic, rather, that many work toward intelligent and compassionate care for all those who suffer from AIDS or who work with AIDS sufferers.

Our role is to work without judgment or condemnation. So, I want to let you know that there are clergy from the different churches who have made an effort to understand and respond to the AIDS crisis, and who do so with compassion and intelligence.

Dr. John M. Raba
Medical Director
Cermak Health Services,
Cook County Department of Corrections

In my capacity as the Medical Director of Cermak Health Services at the Cook County Department of Corrections, I supervise the medical screening and ongoing care delivered to the 55,000-60,000 individuals annually admitted to the Cook County Department of Corrections.

Thirty percent of those incarcerated at the Cook County Department of Corrections are intravenous drug users and consequently overtly at risk for exposure to the Human Immunodeficiency Virus (HIV); another 35-45% participate or have participated in other high-risk behavior – unsafe sex, sex with an intravenous drug user, multiple blood transfusions prior to 1985, etc. To date there has been little concerted effort or programing in the community directed at the minority, low income, low educational background men and women who comprise the majority of individuals entering the urban and metropolitan jails of Cook County and the USA. These individuals have limited knowledge about AIDS and have limited access to conventional sources of health information. A significant proportion of the incarcerated population also falls into groups that are difficult to reach and even more difficult to effectively educate concerning AIDS and its prevention. At this time in our society, correctional staff (police, jails, prisons and their medical personnel) have a unique opportunity to educate and inform this at-risk-for-AIDS population, who come into contact with the judicial system, about this disease and its prevention. Law enforcement and correctional agencies could play an important role in interrupting the spread of AIDS in Chicago, Cook County and throughout the United States of America.

Cermak Health Services has committed its program to teaching detainees entering the Cook County Department of Corrections about the ways of minimizing or eliminating their at-risk-for-AIDS behavior. We presently do **no** screening for HIV antibodies and have no plans to initiate such testing. We feel that antibody screening, in and of itself, is counterproductive and would waste significant funding that could be more effectively spent on health education about AIDS. Each and every admission is given, at the time of entrance, a simply written informational pamphlet about AIDS. A twelve-minute videotape about AIDS and at-risk behavior is shown twice daily on each of the Cook County Department of Corrections' 130 tiers. The videotape was specifically produced for use in our facility and is directed at young, low education, low income urban men and women. With the use of a grant and extended work hours of specially trained members of our mental health team, we provide one-on-one and small-group counseling to high-risk individuals. The counseling has been well received by the detainees and we feel that these educated men and women will infuse preventive information (safe sex, stop the sharing of needles, etc.) back into their home communities when they are discharged from this facility.

It has been frequently stated that inmate populations ostracize and even threaten to kill fellow inmates who are known or rumored to have AIDS, ARC or HIV infection. This has **not** been our experience at the Cook County Department of Corrections where men and women with HIV infection are housed in units with individuals presumed not to be infected. Once it becomes known that an inmate is infected, and indeed little remains secret in the jail setting, there is generally an initial surge of fear on the units – both in the correctional staff and among the inmates. We have found that brief informational group sessions, in which the transmission of AIDS is frankly discussed with the officers, the individual with the HIV infection and the other detainees, quickly resolve the anxiety and fear on the involved tier. To date there have been no acts of violence against men or women with AIDS, ARC or HIV infection because of their disease. We have found that the incarcerated population is indeed open to education about AIDS and will appropriately respond to this information.

Law enforcement and correctional staffs are fully cognizant of the fact that they have frequent contact with certain groups of citizens – intravenous drug users, street walkers – that are engaged in high-risk-for-AIDS activities. However, during the normal course of performing their duties in the correctional field – frisks, shake downs, shackling, restraining uncooperative clients, etc. – police, correctional officers and probation/parole officers are rarely, if ever, exposed to any, even minimal, risk of exposure to the Human Immunodeficiency Virus. I repeatedly inform correctional staff that the greatest risk for exposure to AIDS exists not in their occupational work environment but in their private, particularly their sexual, lives. When I speak to correctional officers, I spend as much or more time reviewing "safe sex" than I do discussing potential on-the-job exposures.

To place this current topic in perspective, I must emphasize that if we really were interested in improving the occupational conditions of law enforcement/correctional personnel that result in short- or long-term illness, even death, we would spend exponentially more money and time on stop-smoking programs. We would minimize the passive exposure of correctional staff to smoke by eliminating smoking in squad cars, offices, tiers, desk stations, etc. We must remember this when we speak of educating staff about AIDS and its prevention. It is not speculation that, at least for the next few decades, more correctional staff will die from or suffer the consequences of smoking or smoke exposure than will be affected with AIDS.

Nonetheless, Acquired Immune Deficiency Syndrome, the disease which prompted the convening of this conference, is a highly lethal disease which threatens all segments of our society. It deserves the tremendous attention that it has been given. The concerns of law enforcement and correctional staffs about their potential occupational exposure to this infection must be addressed. Even though the risk is minimal, we must attempt to make their risk for exposure to HIV virtually zero.

The Cook County Department of Corrections in coordination with Cermak Health Services has an ongoing training program about AIDS, its prevention and potential on-the-job exposure, for all new and veteran correctional officers. Physicians even visit the facility's multiple roll calls to give the officers updated information about AIDS. We train the officers that they must take the same precautions with all detainees whether they know or do not know the detainee's HIV antibody status. We advise them to treat all detainees as if they have AIDS – the same precautions exist for all.

All blood or body fluid is to be considered contaminated – there is no such thing as "clean" blood. The officers are trained not to touch open wounds, not to touch blood, not to touch urine, not to touch any body fluid unless they are properly protected. Deputy Nimocks of the Chicago Police Department said that disposable gloves are now available in all Chicago Police Department vehicles. Gloves are also available on each tier and at each officer's work station in the Cook County Department of Corrections. The Illinois Department of Public Health recently advised all ambulance medics that they should use special one-way air flow masks when they do mouth-to-mouth resuscitation. Even prior to this announcement, we had noted that our correctional officers had a paralyzing reluctance to initiate unprotected mouth-to-mouth resuscitation, not only on inmates, but even on their fellow correctional officers. In order to assure that CPR was immediately and effectively performed in our institution, we purchased one-way CPR masks which are now available in each security office at the Cook County Department of Corrections. The CPR masks are now used in cases of a cardiac or pulmonary arrest. These masks, disposable or not, should be mandatory equipment in all police vehicles, police lockups, jails and prisons.

I strongly advise individuals concerned with this issue to initiate organized instruction of your staffs about AIDS, its transmission, its prevention and occupational precautions. You must regularly monitor the compliance of staff with the protective policies which have been enacted. Ongoing surveillance of the staff will assure that all employees are indeed fully protecting themselves from body fluid exposure in the occupational setting.

All law enforcement agencies and correctional facilities, however, must establish protocols for dealing with staff who are significantly exposed to potentially contaminated blood or body fluids. Needle-sticks do occur while frisking intravenous drug users or searching homes, vehicles or cells. Arresting and correctional officers are indeed bitten by arrestees and detainees; staff are splashed by the blood of wounded or injured clients. The guidelines of the Centers for Disease Control (CDC) should be followed in determining what testing and medical advice needs to be performed. Appropriate counseling must be given to all law enforcement, correctional officers and arrestees/detainees who are exposed to blood or body fluids. Law enforcement, correctional officers and others may need to practice safe sex, even with their spouses, until they are advised by medical personnel that they have not been infected with HIV due to their exposure to another's body fluids. At all times, the rights of confidentiality must be fully protected for both the in-volved officer and the arrestee/detainee. The State of Illinois laws concerning confidentiality must be diligently followed.

Within our facility, I tell the correctional staff that their greatest risk for on-the-job exposure is from human bites but not the bites that occur during routine restraining action. I speak of the tooth-induced injury which occurs when an officer, justified or not, hits a detainee in the mouth and subsequently lacerates his own hand. The blood or body fluid of the inmate contaminates the officer's open wound; the blood from the officer's hand injury enters the not-uncommonly cut mouth or lips of the detainee. Both are exposed to potentially contaminated blood – both need to be screened for HIV infection, counseled and practice safe sex for at least six months. This type of exposure is absolutely preventable and must be stopped. Any educational program about AIDS and its prevention for law enforcement personnel must clearly identify this risk to its officers. Those of you attending this conference must relay this important information back to your fellow officers. All movement of an officer's hands toward an arrestee's or detainee's mouth must be avoided. During the last three (3) years at the Cook County De-partment of Corrections, this has been the leading cause of our correctional staff being exposed to blood. This at-risk behavior can be eliminated through education, peer pressure and proper supervi-sion.

Finally, I strongly advise all law enforcement and correctional facilities that they must be administratively prepared for the day when a police, parole, probation or correctional officer is diagnosed as having been infected, either from occupational or personal life exposure, with the Human Immunodeficiency Virus. You must have policies in place that deal with the allowed work assignment of an HIV-infected officer. I personally know of no circumstance in which an officer would need to have his/her duties limited because of this infection. However, you may come under significant political pressure from your elected boards to do something quite different. I feel that if you have educated the infected individual's fellow officers, they will readily accept him/her in the work environment and if you have established reasonable, medically sound policies to guide your decisions in this matter, you will be well positioned to legally and politically defend your decisions.

In summary, education and re-education (about AIDS and its prevention) of law enforcement and correctional officers, arrestees, detainees and inmates are the unqualified key to the management of this dreaded disease in the correctional setting. Communities that commit appropriate funding to the education of staff and clients of their judicial and correctional systems will play a vital role in interrupting the spread of Human Immunodeficiency Virus.

JoAnne Ross
Correctional Health Services Coordinator
Illinois Department of Corrections

We began our AIDS program in 1984. Our program has been developed under the direction of the department's Medical Director, Ronald Shansky, M.D. Dr. Shansky is a board-certified internist, a member of the Governor's Interdisciplinary Advisory Council on AIDS and is renowned in the area of correctional health care.

The Illinois Department of Corrections has four (4) adult reception centers. Eighty percent of all inmates who enter the system come from the Chicago-Cook County area and are received at our Reception Center in Joliet. The first part of our program involves a comprehensive history and physical examination of each inmate at each reception center. All of our physicians have been instructed to look for clinical manifestations such as chronic diarrhea, reoccurring sore throats, fevers, sudden weight loss and other manifestations discussed by the earlier speakers. In taking the history of inmates we include questions relevant to high-risk behavior such as IV drug use. We also do a laboratory workup on every inmate, which includes a white blood count to assist us in identifying individuals at high risk. Inmates found to have a low white blood count, a history of IV drug use, a history of sharing needles with a known AIDS victim or other high-risk behavior, combined with clinical manifestations such as chronic diarrhea or enlarged lymph glands, are put in our high-risk surveillance program. Inmates classified as high risk are examined every three months and a white blood count is repeated. Should the white blood count be very low, the physician would look further at the immune system by doing cell-immunity studies and T-cell studies.

We do **no** mass screening of any kind. We preface this by saying that we assume that everyone is infected and we are encouraging risk-reducing behavior through education and training.

We test on an individual basis only when there is an unusual incident; for example, an altercation or sexual assault takes place which might involve an exchange of bodily fluids. The HIV test is offered to the individual, who has the right to refuse. This test is given at the time of the incident and at intervals of three, six and nine months.

The second part of our program consists of training and education. We have a very comprehensive program for both the staff and the inmates. Every inmate, adult and juvenile, who comes into the system receives AIDS education and training. Each employee who comes to the department receives AIDS training as part of our pre-service orientation program.

Each correctional institution is responsible for holding monthly training sessions on AIDS. These programs must do more than just show films. We have encouraged a one-on-one exchange and good communication about the various topics mentioned by Dr. Hammett. Trainers and all medical staff must attend AIDS Update Training at least once a year, or more often if new information becomes available.

It is interesting to note that the inmates have been more receptive to training and education than the staff. It must be stated, also, that those who are most upset are primarily those staff members who do not have day-to-day contact with inmates.

Since 1984, when the Department of Corrections began to monitor and look at AIDS, we have had a total of nine confirmed cases of AIDS: eight males and one female. Of that total we had seven deaths and two are now on parole. Five were IV drug users who had come from the New York area, where shooting galleries are common. We currently have approximately 90 residents in our high-risk surveillance program and five confirmed ARC cases.

To sum up, the department has established well-defined policies and procedures concerning AIDS with special emphasis on education and training for our security staff, medical staff and inmates. We also make counseling available to all inmates before they are discharged or placed on parole. The inmates see a counselor and are given information about testing and counseling available through the Illinois Department of Public Health.

Caryn Berman
Associate Director of Clinical Services
Travelers and Immigrants Aid of Chicago

From a community/social work perspective, the AIDS epidemic demands a partnership between multidisciplined professionals and institutions for prevention and support services. No matter whether the target population is living within the community setting or moving through the courts or correctional facilities, we must have consistent messages and common perspectives for effectively managing the epidemic. We must also continue to develop programs with respect to the compatibility and cooperation between law enforcement agencies, correctional facilities and community groups. As Mr. Grossman said this morning, "It is **our** problem."

When it comes to AIDS, there is no boundary line that separates us, the professionals, from them, the clients or detainees. If you had sex in the last 10 years, you must assess your risk for exposure to HIV.

Staff anxiety and fear of AIDS must be addressed before asking staff members to educate inmates or work with HIV-infected persons. Staff concern about occupational risk of HIV infection is usually unfounded. The point that must be repeated is that personal risk is incurred through sexual contact and/or needle sharing, which I assume are **not** job functions. We, the professionals, need AIDS education, and we in turn are responsible for educating and working with those in our charge.

When we talk about AIDS and HIV we are talking about sex, drug use and death. My professional education did not prepare me to cope intimately with any of these topics. I learned theories about death and dying, substance abuse, and sexuality. In the field, on the job, and in our personal lives we learn the meaning behind the theories. Most of us are personally, not just professionally, unprepared for the intimate and sensitive counseling necessitated by the AIDS epidemic. Our spiritual, religious and/or moral values may be in conflict with our professional responsibilities. This conflict requires that we speak with our colleagues, attend seminars and training sessions, and dialogue with friends, family and professionals in order to train ourselves. We need to develop consistent, concerted efforts to work with the issues of sexuality, drug use and death in ways that do not harm the client.

Peer Counseling

Peer counseling is an effective means of delivering AIDS education. Dr. Raba mentioned that a person from within the unit talking to his/her colleagues has a more profound and credible impact than someone from outside the system. Whether the target population is inmates or law enforcement personnel, peer counselors need to be trained from within the client group. Training inmates to educate and counsel other inmates develops and reinforces a peer culture for AIDS prevention.

At Travelers and Immigrants Aid, our Neon Street Center for Youth has found peer counseling to be especially effective in reaching street hustlers. We developed an outreach program in which we train a couple of adolescents who have lived on the streets to talk to other adolescents about the risk of AIDS. Have you noticed how willing inmates and other client groups are to believe their compadres, their peers, over the word of experts? Use that observation for choosing a messenger for AIDS education who has the trust and support of his/her audience.

The community social service agencies work directly with the inmates, as well as with their families, sometimes before and often after incarceration. Those family members may be the inmates' sexual and/or drug partners or their children and may be at risk of HIV infection due to the inmates' HIV status. The friend or family member may also be the past or future transmitter of the HIV virus to the inmate. When it comes to AIDS, there is no boundary line.

Case Management & Treatment Plans

Inmates and/or their family members lack financial and emotional resources for coping with the epidemic. Many inmates do not have family or peers who would support them in event of illness. Drug users often feed their habit by ripping off those around them. Developing case management and treatment plans that are feasible and can be implemented upon discharge from the hospital or prison is ideal but not necessarily attainable. It will be difficult to find all the necessary components of a support system to meet the physical and mental health needs of the HIV-infected, as well as their concrete needs for shelter and food. The problems we face in planning for the HIV-infected inmate or prison releasee in the community are shared by others with AIDS or ARC: the lack of resources for a continuity of care. Locally in Chicago, and nationally, we are stymied in our efforts to admit patients with AIDS/ARC into extended care facilities, hence the retention of patients in the acute care setting.

There is a need for more preventive and supportive counseling directed at law enforcement personnel, detainees and inmates. There is a need for repeated counseling and education, as well as case management services for those infected with HIV; and there is a need for community resources to assist individuals and families in coping with the illness.

Theodore Hammett, Ph.D.
Associate, Abt Associates

In regard to education and training, we just heard about the importance of the peer counseling model. This applies, as well, to the education and training of staff in criminal justice agencies. It may be useful to involve the representatives of an audience in developing the training, so that they can help to shape the content of the training program.

There is a need to evaluate the effectiveness of training and education programs. This can be achieved by administering pre- and post-surveys to see how much of the message has been absorbed and retained.

Regarding overall policy development, a few points need to be reinforced. Policy regarding precautionary measures must be rational and appropriate to the actual level of risk involved. It must be applied to all people in a consistent way. As Harvey Grossman mentioned, the precautionary measures that are taken must reinforce rather than undermine the necessary educational message about AIDS. That is a very important point that needs to be repeated. Also, a cautionary word about precautionary measures and policies is in order. No matter how good a policy is or how comprehensive it is, it cannot apply to each and every situation. This is simply impossible. Just as in so many other ways, law enforcement and criminal justice professionals must exercise good judgment and discretion.

As far as testing is concerned, it should be emphasized that testing people is not in itself a solution to the problem of AIDS. Simply testing people does not solve the problem. For instance, if a testing program is to be undertaken, one should know with great specificity how the information will be used; and, one must decide how having this information will affect behavior. Will the information help people do their jobs better? That is a very key question to ask.

Finally, there are some legal and liability issues to be touched on briefly. These relate to correctional agencies as well as other criminal justice agencies. There has been an explosion of litigation on AIDS in correctional settings in the past few years. These cases have challenged the quality of care, both correctional and medical. There have been cases brought by inmates who demanded mass screening of all inmates in the system. There have also been cases brought by inmates who had been segregated and have challenged that segregation on the basis of equal protection and other constitutional provisions. There are also a number of potential legal issues and liability issues that have not as yet been the subject of litigation.

Training programs can protect agencies against these liability problems. For example, if a police officer became infected with HIV in an incident on the job and if that officer, in the course of that incident, had failed to take precautionary measures that would ordinarily be indicated, and, if the officer could demonstrate that he/she had not been properly trained by the department in those precautionary measures, there might be a liability problem for the department.

Obviously the major reason for training is to enable people to protect themselves and to act rationally and reasonably. But departments also wish to avoid liability, and conducting training is important for that reason as well.

The training issue comes up in many legal matters. In an administrative action involving a correctional officer in Minnesota in which the correctional officer refused to carry out a search of an inmate out of fear of becoming infected with HIV, the correctional system attempted to discharge that employee for failing to do his duty. The employee pointed to an unclear training message that had been given to him in the course of training by the corrections department, which in effect said "We really don't know how this infection is transmitted, so be careful." This is a very unclear and misleading statement. Because the department had failed to provide clear and accurate education, its action in discharging the employee was disallowed. This example, once again, underlines the importance of providing accurate training and education for criminal justice staff.

Highlights of Questions and Answers

Question:

Should correctional authorities provide condoms to inmates to reduce the risk involved in sexual activity within jails and prisons?

Hammett:

A few correctional institutions are making condoms available in their facilities. The Vermont Department of Corrections is one such institution. This received some national publicity last spring when the policy was announced. In New York City there is a special unit for gay inmates where condoms are made available, too. This policy is about to be extended throughout the entire New York City jail system. And, in several other institutions condoms are distributed to inmates prior to furloughs or conjugal visits that might be granted.

This is a highly charged question for correctional institutions because if they do make condoms available it may appear that they are condoning or even encouraging sexual activity. The Vermont Department of Corrections responded to this argument by saying that they were not making any judgment about the behavior itself but were simply acknowledging that sexual relations are occurring within the institutions and that from a public health standpoint they have an obligation to take steps that will reduce the transmission of this virus. This seems to be a fairly compelling argument.

Question:

Regarding the issue of confidentiality, do counselors have the responsibility of notifying the sexual partners of known AIDS victims?

Hammett:

There is a CDC (Centers for Disease Control) recommendation for public health care workers who counsel infected people. According to these guidelines, infected people have the responsibility to notify their sexual partners. If they are unwilling to notify their partners or if there is doubt that their partners will seek counseling, confidential procedures should be used to assure that the partners are notified.

This is a very sensitive issue. What it means is that in the event a person who is being counseled refuses to notify his/her sexual partner(s), the counselor may then have a moral obligation to take steps to notify those people.

There are legal issues involved here, too. There are many states and jurisdictions in which such notification is illegal.

Berman:

This is a very controversial topic. Many community agencies and correctional facilities face this dilemma. It is important to work through the person who has the disease and motivate him/her to tell his/her risk partners. Time is the enemy as we work against the clock to help the client with the disease assume responsibility before the next person becomes infected. Our goal should be to get everyone to assume self-responsibility. We should get everyone to say, "I am responsible for my body," and to look out for his/her self-interests in following safe sex and other health guidelines for reducing the risk of exposure to HIV.

Question:

How does one overcome employee resistance to taking precautions?

Berman:

The answer lies in education and training. Caution should be used in any risk situation. Repetitious training of staff is important. "Once is not enough" is a good motto for AIDS education.

The need for intervention advocacy should also be recognized at the staff level. Addressing staff concerns and collegial resistance is just as important as directing one's efforts toward inmates and/or clients who may be infected. We must look at the internal systems that are either inconsistent or are sabotaging our programs for education.

Question:

Should police officers wear gloves when they deal with people? How are police officers going to accept this?

Raba:

Procedures should call for use of gloves whenever there is exposure to body fluids. Everyone – police officers, dentists, physicians, etc. – should wear gloves in such a situation.

People should be educated and trained as widely as possible so they do not overreact.

Afterword

Compassion is demanded. It must be an informed compassion filled with the knowledge of the reality described by the women and men, all experts in their fields, who have contributed to this document.

These experts have not lost their critical stance with regard to the issues of justice and care, i.e., the interface of AIDS and the law enforcement community. They are well aware that the AIDS debate carries with it "... concern about a deadly epidemic...(with) the potential to affect social policy through the rest of the twentieth century and beyond." At the same time each of these experts offers specific information – information for self-protection, for the protection of systems and institutions and for the protection of those within the community whose lives are directly touched by this deadly virus.

Years ago, Reinhold Niebuhr wrote:

"Politics will, to the end of history, be an area where conscience and power meet, where the ethical and coercive factors of human life will interpenetrate and work out their tentative and uneasy compromises."

We are struggling to be just. We are struggling to be humane and ethical in our treatment of everyone, including ourselves. Unfortunately, ignorance and fear often coerce us in directions that are neither ethical nor humane. What these experts have done is stimulate our growth process so that at that place where law enforcement and AIDS "interpenetrate," justice and care, though threatened, will not cease but will abound.

Biographical Notes

Gad J. Bensinger is professor and chairman of the Criminal Justice Department at Loyola University of Chicago. Before joining Loyola University in 1977, he was director of the Cook County Criminal Justice Training and Leadership Development Program. He earned his Ph.D. in 1971 at Loyola University of Chicago.

Caryn Berman is the AIDS coordinator in the office of Health Services at The University of Illinois in Chicago. Previous to that she was the Associate Director of Clinical Services for Travelers and Immigrants Aid of Chicago, where she developed an AIDS program for homeless children and adults, as well as an AIDS education program for persons released from prison. Ms. Berman holds a Master's Degree in Social Service Administration from The University of Chicago.

Harvey Grossman is the legal director of the Chicago Office of the American Civil Liberties Union. He is a member of the Illinois AIDS Disciplinary Advisory Council and chairs the legal sub-group. He is also a member of the ACLU National AIDS Task Force. Mr. Grossman holds a J.D. from Northwestern University School of Law.

Theodore Hammett is an associate of Abt Associates, a large social policy research firm in Cambridge, MA. He serves as a consultant to the U.S. Justice Department's National Institute of Justice and the National Institute of Corrections. He has published three major publications on AIDS: *AIDS in Corrections Facilities: Issues and Options; AIDS and the Law Enforcement Officer: Concerns and Policy Responses*; and *AIDS in Prisons and Jails*. Dr. Hammett is a member of the American Correctional Association's Task Force on AIDS. He holds a B.A. from Harvard University and a Ph.D. from Brandeis University.

Rudolph Nimocks is Deputy Superintendent of the Chicago Police Department in charge of the Bureau of Administrative Services, overseeing such divisions as finance, personnel and training. Previous to that he headed the Organized Crime Division with citywide responsibility for investigations. Deputy Superintendent Nimocks holds a Master's Degree in Public Administration from the Illinois Institute of Technology, Chicago.

Dr. Paul O'Keefe is chief of the Infectious Disease Section of the Loyola University Stritch School of Medicine in Maywood, Illinois. He is also an associate professor of medicine at the Stritch Medical School. He holds an M.D. from the Loyola University School of Medicine.

Dr. John A. Raba is the medical director of Cermak Health Services, Cook County Department of Corrections. He is also Attending Physician of Internal Medicine at Cook County Hospital. Dr. Raba is at the forefront in educating staff and inmates about risk reduction and AIDS. Dr. Raba holds an M.D. from the Northwestern University School of Medicine.

JoAnne Ross is coordinator of health services in the Illinois Department of Corrections. She is responsible for maintaining the department's statistical data on the High Risk Surveillance Program. She has written the department's *Directory on AIDS* and also developed its *Manual on AIDS*.

Cyprian Lamar Rowe, F.M.S., M.S.W., Ph.D., is a Marist Brother. He is an assistant professor in the Graduate School of Social Work at Loyola University of Chicago.

Rev. George P. Winchester, S.J., is Director of Ministry at Loyola University of Chicago, Water Tower Campus. A campus minister at Loyola since 1981, he was previously at Boston College. He is a member of Loyola's Committee on Infectious Diseases. He earned graduate degrees in philosophy, theology, and English from Boston College, Weston School of Theology and Middlebury College, respectively.

Suggested Readings

Hammett, Theodore M. <u>AIDS and the Law Enforcement Officer:
Concerns and Policy Responses</u>. Washington, D.C.:
National Institute of Justice, 1987.

Hammett, Theodore M. <u>AIDS in Correctional Facilities: Issues and
Options</u>. Washington, D.C.:
National Institute of Justice, 1987.

Laszlo, Anna, and Ayres, Marilyn. <u>AIDS: Improving the Response
of the Correctional System</u>. Alexandria, Virginia:
National Sheriff's Association, 1986.

National Sheriff's Association. <u>Acquired Immune Deficiency
Syndrome: 100 Questions and Answers</u>. Alexandria, Virginia:
National Sheriff's Association, 1987.